GOD'S MEDICINE OF FAITH — THE WORD

by NORVEL HAYES

published by
Hunter Books
201 McClellan Road
Kingwood, Texas 77339

Scripture quotations are taken from:
The Authorized King James Version

ISBN 0-917726-20-0

CONTENTS

CHAPTER I

CHAPTER II

CHAPTER III

PREFACE

This faith-building book by Norvel Hayes presents God's Word, applied in faith, as a sufficient prescription to meet any need, regardless of how great it may seem. Its title is unique, but fascinating.

It is not likely that anyone can read this book without receiving an answer to his prayers as each sentence of faith pierces, penetrates, and activates the human mind to believe for the miraculous.

Norvel Hayes is a very successful businessman, and is the founder of Campus Challenge, the organizer of Christian training centers, and the author of many books. He is a world-known lay teacher who spends most of his time traveling and teaching in faith seminars and ministering deliverance and healing.

His style is direct, simple and full of life and excitement. His teachings inspire his listeners to confess and act their faith with remarkable results. The anointing of God's power rests upon him heavily as he challenges Christians to return to the unadulterated Word of God and to take it at face value. As you read his books or hear him speak, it will be obvious to you that he is a chosen vessel, a servant of God, who was called as a successful businessman to do even a greater work in God's business to bring deliverance to those who are bound and oppressed by the enemy.

Although he does not make any pretense of a scholarly or precise literary style, no one can read or hear his simple teachings without being convinced that here is a sincere man who is determined to make a mark for Christ and his great kingdom here on earth. Norvel realizes that the work of Christ's church is to help build the Kingdom of God, and he is surely doing his part to carry out that command in his various and constant ministries.

Let God bless you and advance you in your part of God's business as you take this "medicine."

Rev. H. M. M. Keele

GOD'S "MEDICINE" OF FAITH —
THE WORD

CHAPTER I
A Sure Cure

This may seem to be a strange title, but it is a subject which God gave me as the result of a study of two main thoughts which are taken from both the Old and New Testaments. As an earthly physician prescribes medicine which is sometimes bitter to take, so God's Word often seems bitter and hard to imbibe and spiritually digest, but if we want our needs met, we must "take as prescribed." If we fail to heed his Word, let us not think that we will receive anything from the Lord.

Please turn to the 11th chapter of Hebrews, verse 1. Let me remind you that you must have faith in God to receive answers to your prayers. You may say, "I do have faith. I believe that God can do anything." That still is not good enough because your faith has to be active. If you say that God can do anything, and you end up doing nothing, then you won't receive your answers. You must remember that in receiving things from God there are TWO parts to play. God has his part to perform, but you also have your part to perform.

God's part is to release the power because God has the power. You are just as I am in this respect. You have no power of your own. God has all power on earth and in heaven, but there are laws by which God's power is released. Just as there are laws in the natural, there are also laws in the spiritual realm.

Sir Isaac Newton, an English philosopher and mathematician who formulated the basic laws of dynamics and the law of gravity, was said to have been lying under an apple tree one day. An apple fell and hit him on the head. He began to wonder why the apple didn't fall up instead of down. As the result of this he began to do some study and research.

He discovered that there is a natural pull of things toward the center of the earth, and this caused him to come up with the law of gravity, which of course is a natural law created by God to keep things on the earth. Without this law, we'd float around in the air like a balloon with gas in it. That is why things fall down instead of up and why they fall over easily. It is a law that affects the entire universe, and consequently the human race.

One day soon when Christ comes to take his bride away, the holy, born-again saints of God who are looking for him will discover that the law of gravity will be reversed, but only for them. The same God who made the laws has power to reverse them! His spiritual laws of power transcend the natural or physical laws and take precedence over them.

Likewise there are spiritual laws which affect the entire race. These laws cannot be revoked or refuted. They must be learned and adhered to and acted upon by the human race if there is to be the divine result of God working in hearts and lives. The Bible gives these laws very simply and plainly, but the majority of people either don't read them, don't comprehend them, or don't believe them. They are found in God's law book, the

Word of God, as given in the Old and New Testaments.

God has all power in heaven and on earth. Heaven may seem far away to you or just a mythical place, but heaven is just as real as earth is. I know, because one time God allowed me to go there and see a part of it. It was the part where the little infants live. It is a beautiful place, too lovely to describe in our earthly vocabulary; it is a paradise! The grass and flowers were many, many times more beautiful than what we see here. There were no stinging or poisonous insects. The apples and other fruit didn't decay because there was no death or no worms to eat them. If there had been a worm he would have just crawled around in peace as everything there is peaceful and in perfect harmony.

We can't afford to miss heaven. We must remember that in the beginning this world was like heaven until Satan entered in and deceived Adam and Eve. Heaven is just as real as this earth. God simply reached out and with little effort He SPAKE IT INTO EXISTENCE.

What I want you to realize is that God's Word is still just as powerful and he can still speak things into existence if we have the faith to believe. Heaven is the throne or headquarters of God. Jesus is there right now listening to every word that you and I say. He is our High Priest; he is our MEDIATOR. That means he is the one who makes the connection to God for us. When Stephen was being stoned to death for telling the truth, he declared just before his soul took its departure from his body that he saw Jesus standing at THE RIGHT HAND OF THE FATHER (Acts 7:55). Just as Stephen saw him there, he is still there, interceding for you and me and will be until he comes back for God's children.

Jesus is watching and is listening to you and when you diligently seek him and believe his Word, and your faith passes his test, then God releases his power to you. You may say, "What kind of power?" I say, "Any kind of power that you want for any need that you have." God's power will actually be manifested on this earth in behalf of your needs, to meet those needs, regardless of what they are, as long as the things you are asking for are in God's will and if they are best for you in every way. God is a FAITH GOD and you can only approach him by FAITH. That is his law, that you have faith. There is no other way to approach God and no other way to get your prayers answered. That may seem to be strong "medicine" to take spiritually, but it is God's prescription for results! The Bible is God's medicine to the Christian. Glory be to God forevermore!

In the natural, if you had a physical need and you went to your physician and he said, "You can never be well unless you take this medicine," if you wanted to live, and had faith in the doctor, and the medicine, you would take it. You wouldn't go pay a pharmacist a lot to have the prescription filled, then put it on the shelf. If you did, you might as well not have gone to the doctor in the first place. But if you're the kind of a person who has lots of faith in medical science, you'd take the medicine because you have confidence in the doctor's knowledge.

When we come to Christ we not only have to get our needs diagnosed, but we must get HIS "prescription," which is the Word of

God. It will meet every need. We have a part to do. Our part is to take his "medicine," spiritually speaking, whether we like it or not. Sometimes it won't taste good, especially if God shows us our faults, weak points, and shortcomings. We have to face up to the fact that we are sick and we must meet his laws or requirements. In other words, we have to take his "medicine," which is his Word, and it will correct any inconsistencies, sins, or lack of faith and heal us physically, mentally or emotionally, depending on what our needs are. BUT WE HAVE TO TAKE HIS MEDI- CINE – THE WORD! The Word is God's medicine!

Just as the medicine destroys disease and brings healing, so God's Word, when applied or taken into our hearts, destroys sin and increases our faith, and brings whatever healing we need. If we do not have confidence in his Word, then we don't even need to go to him because it won't do us any more good than if after going to a doctor we refuse to take his medicine. The great difference between Jesus, the Great Physician, and any earthly physician is that our doctor sometimes diagnoses the case wrong, or gives the wrong medicine, or the medicine doesn't really help. With Jesus it is different. He knows exactly what is wrong with us and his Word always heals and brings perfect results IF WE TAKE IT AS PRESCRIBED.

Faith has to be "fed," or nourished. By that I mean it has to be acted upon and acknowledged by our mouths, because *"Faith, if it hath not works, is dead, being alone."* *(James 2:17)*. Unless you act right, talk right, talk your faith, it will die. This doesn't apply only to healing, but to our financial and other needs. We must act and talk faith!

Hebrews 11:1 states, *"Now faith is the substance of things hoped for, the evidence of things not seen."* That means faith for now, not yesterday, not tomorrow, but faith right now! God is the God of the present. When Moses was told by God to go deliver the Hebrew children from the cruel Egyptian bondage, the Lord said to tell the wicked Pharaoh that "I AM THE TRUE GOD," send him. What does that mean?

In the rules and laws of grammar, "am" is present tense. It means right now at the present time. God gave this title of himself to

Moses to let him know that he was not only the God of the past, or of the future, but always OF THE PRESENT TIME-NOW! He wanted Moses to remember this so that each time he faced a new problem or crisis, he would remember that he was present at that very minute to meet the needs of Moses and the children of Israel, and he was! NOW always puts him in the present. If we don't realize he is a NOW God and if we don't have NOW FAITH, then we will always put the answers to our prayers in the future and the answer will never come. It has been said that procrastination is a thief of time. It is also a destroyer of faith.

What is substance? It is something that is tangible, not something which cannot be seen or touched. So faith is not just dreaming or wishful thinking; it is actually the substance of things hoped for. It can be good health, life or prosperity, but first it has to be claimed and confessed before its results are seen. It is real! It is alive, so it has to be active. Just as you can't see the yeast in the dough that causes it to rise from a small wad of dough to a large, delicious loaf of bread, so you can't see faith, but it is ACTIVE. It is acting or doing its work all the time. AC-TION FAITH IS THE ANSWER TO ALL OUR NEEDS!

You may ask, "Can you be healed by faith?" Of course you can, if you really want to be healed, even if the doctor says it is an incurable disease. You may ask, "Can faith raise the dead?" Of course it can, if you don't want to give that person up to death, and it is not time for that person to go. Many ministers and missionaries have witnessed that they have seen the dead raised. Of course, this doesn't happen real often, but there are documented proofs that it has happened. It is God's power through Christ that does it. This power is the same as when Jesus was on earth and raised the dead. It hasn't decreased. When you read the gospels, you don't think it is ridiculous or presumptuous to believe that he raised the dead. Well, it still isn't because he is the SAME LORD! St. John 14:12 declares, *"Verily, verily, I say unto you, He that believeth on me, the works that I do SHALL HE DO ALSO; and greater works than these shall he do; because I go unto my Father."* Jesus was not joking; he meant what he said.

note

A friend gives the following testimony: "Before my second child was born, a very spiritual lady minister, and also my father, were warned that I would die while my child was being born. They did not tell me this as they were afraid they might frighten or upset me, but they both left their homes in different cities in California and came to be with me during that time.

"When my son was born, I actually did die. My spirit left my body. Later on the nurses told me there was absolutely no pulse for several minutes.

"I was suddenly hurled as if thrown into an intense darkness, so dark that it could be felt, but as quickly as I hit this darkness, which I realized was the 'valley of death,' Jesus appeared to me like a flash of lightning. Light was emanating from his presence. Had it not been for that light I would have continued to be in total darkness.

"He took me by the hand and walked with me for a long time. I can remember that I felt so unworthy that he should walk with me that I would scarcely raise my head to behold his beautiful face and long, white, iridescent robe. Tears trickled down my cheeks as I saw the ugly scars in his sandaled feet. I kept thinking of his words of warning to those who reject him in this life and fail to be cleansed of their sins by his precious blood. He said such people would be cast into outer darkness where there is weeping and wailing and gnashing of teeth.

"As I looked out into that terrible darkness, from which there can never be a return to those who do not have Christ in their lives, there were no words great or powerful enough to express my gratitude and thanks to Jesus for dying to save a lost world from that place, if they will only accept him as the TRUE LIGHT.

"After we had walked for what seemed to be several minutes, I looked up and saw a beautiful paradise at the end of the 'valley of death.' It was as if I was looking through the porthole of a ship into a great and glorious beyond.

"Back at home, my precious father and my elderly lady friend, who was the minister, had been told that I was dead, but they would not accept it as they knew my work on earth in winning souls was not finished and that my little five-year-old daughter needed me; also that if my newly-born baby son lived, he would need me, so they would not let death be the victor. In the name of Jesus they demanded that life come into my body, and they believed what they said! Like a flash, I suddenly came back to the same place I had originally come from.

"The next thing I knew was that my spirit entered my body; then I heard the cries of my newly-born baby. When I came to, I was talking about the beauties of heaven and of my lovely Savior. I opened my eyes to see three nurses and a doctor hovering over me. It seems the doctor had already given me up. Jesus decided to let me live because two people refused to let me go.

"That experience is still as vivid and real to me as if it happened yesterday. Since then I have never feared death because I know Jesus will be there to take me safely across. He is the light of my life now. He will be my LIGHT through all of eternity. JESUS IS THE LIGHT AND THE LIFE!"

We must TALK OUR FAITH AND ACT UPON OUR FAITH. Not only do you have to TALK as if you already have the answer, you must constantly ACT as if you already had the answer. If you don't TALK it and ACT it, then you aren't really believing. You may say, "Well, I haven't received it, but I am still hoping for it."

Hope is not faith! Anyone can hope, but hope rarely brings results, especially when there is need for a miracle. Jesus declared in Mark 11:24: *"What things soever ye desire, WHEN YE PRAY, believe that ye receive them, and ye shall have them."* He didn't mean later, but WHEN YOU PRAY — at that very instant! You can't just hope or wish, you MUST BELIEVE the minute that you pray.

Hebrews 11:6 states, *"But without faith it is impossible to please him: for he that cometh to God must believe that he is, and that he is a rewarder of them that DILIGENTLY SEEK HIM."* Take very special notice of the word diligently. That word means taking heed, persevering, being careful and pursuing with great effort. So, unless we are in earnest and really mean business with God and are determined to hear from him, then there is no need to come at all because he does not want a half-hearted approach.

"Ye have not, because ye ask not" (James 4:2). I know a man who was overseas and wanted to come home, but he didn't have the money. He'd been praying for a long time. One day he became impatient and said, "God, why don't you give me the money to go home? I want to go home!"

God said, "You haven't really asked me in faith, believing."

He said, "I'll correct that, Lord." So he met the condition and took the prescribed cure for his failure, the Word of God. As he really started believing God's Word, God answered and sent him the money for this ticket. It was about five miles to the boat, and he had no means of travel except to walk. After he had walked about three miles he became very tired and said, "God, why didn't you give me enough money to get to the boat also?"

The Lord said to him, "Because you didn't ask me for it. You only asked me to send money for the boat ticket."

It would have been just as easy for him to ask for enough money to meet all his needs, but his faith was not strong enough. God works according to our faith!

A Good Prescription

James 1:6-7 states: *"But let him ask IN FAITH, NOTHING WAVERING. For he that wavereth is like a wave of the sea driven with the wind and tossed. For let not that man think that he shall receive any thing of the Lord."*

If we begin to doubt for just a minute, our faith wavers. You may say, "But that is hard!" Yes, it may be hard not to waver, and this verse may seem like strong "medicine" to take, but it was given to warn us that if we waver and doubt God's Word, we are allowing the enemy of our soul to make us doubt.

This does not please God. Why? Because when we vacillate from belief to unbelief, back and forth, as the waves of the sea, it is because we are double-minded, that is, our mind is divided about whom we are going to believe, God or the devil. God's Word says God's promises are for us; the devil says they are not, and your mind is like two minds if you try to believe them both, so it is a double mind. Verse 8 states, *"A double minded man is unstable in all his ways."* Unbelief affects our entire personality.

God wanted me to share this message, "God's Medicine of Faith — the Word," with you because there are two main "doses" you will have to take to get healed of the cause of your failures. Let's notice carefully and apply the "medicine" of God's Word, as it is powerful to cure and meet our needs. Remember, YOUR FAITH MUST NOT WAVER! Take this dose with care!

Some people say, "Well, I don't have any faith." Yes, you do, because the Bible says that God has dealt to every man the measure of faith (See Romans 12:3). Faith is belief in something. Faith in one sense can be negative as well as positive. You can believe that your prayers are not going to be answered. YOU ARE BELIEVING SOMETHING, but you're believing the wrong thing. You are taking the wrong medicine. You're listening to the voice of the <u>devil</u> and believing him, because <u>it is</u> he, and <u>none other, who puts doubts about</u> <u>God into your mind.</u> So, you have faith in the negative when you should have faith in the positive. You have faith in the devil's thoughts or messages to you. "Strong medicine," you say. Yes, it is, but it is true. <u>No</u> <u>wonder we can't please God if we don't have</u> <u>faith, because that means we are pleasing the</u> *Note* <u>devil when we are doubting God.</u>

A Young Man's Faith Is Rewarded

There is a story which is being told about an aunt and her two nephews who lived in the South. She loved these two young men very much and had taken great pride in them since they were children. When they grew up she promised them that if they would finish college and make satisfactory grades, she would give each of them a lovely, new sports car.

One nephew became discouraged after his first year of college and said to himself, "My aunt won't really keep her word. She's just joking or pulling a prank on us to get us to go to school." He gave up.

The time of graduation came. The other nephew, who had been persistent and faithful in his studies, marched down the aisle with the other graduates and received his diploma. When he came out of the auditorium there sat two beautiful new sports cars near the entrance. The other nephew, who had given up, looked at one of the cars wishfully, knowing that it had been bought for him. He hoped his aunt would change her mind and give him the keys to it, but to his surprise and disappointment, she only waved good-bye and got into the car and drove away, seemingly very nonchalant toward his disappointment. But she was equally disappointed because her nephew did not trust her integrity and did not have enough faith in her words to work for his reward.

"God is no respecter of persons" (*Acts 10:34*). He loves us all the same; he give us all the same chance, but if we fail to accept

and believe and put our belief into action, then he will not reward a doubting Christian. It is only those who will BELIEVE GOD AND ACT UPON HIS WORD THAT WILL HAVE THEIR NEEDS MET. We only fool ourselves if we think it can come any other way. Strong medicine? Yes! But the Great Physician won't change his prescription: HIS LAWS ARE PERFECT.

Sometimes people want to make it appear that God is unjust. During one of my question and answer sessions, which I usually conduct at the end of my teaching messages, I had a person ask me about the heathen who have never been told about God. He wanted to know if God would punish them or if they would be lost. God's Word says, *"He shall judge among the heathen" (Psalm 110:6)*. His judgments are righteous. God judges us according to what we know. I believe that God puts a conscience even in the heathen so that they know if they are doing right or wrong. But that is not for us to worry about. God's Word declares, *"For unto whomsoever much is given, of him shall much be required" (Luke 12:48)*. The heathen may not be judged in the same manner as those who know all of God's Word, but he will be judged according to what he knows.

Many of the Indians, who had never seen a white man nor read a book until America began to be settled, still believed in a God and a supreme creator, whom they called "The Great Spirit." Many also had high moral standards, higher than some people today who dare to call themselves Christian, and they were faithful in their worship of this great spirit. God will judge them according to what they knew. Others worshipped the elements. God condemns those who worship anything made by him whether it be an angel, another person, or the natural elements.

We don't have to worry about God being unjust. We do have to be concerned about ourselves as to whether we are serving him and taking his spiritual "medicine" — his Word — and applying it to our lives to make sure that our souls are saved and our bodies healed so we can serve him better.

It is our duty and obligation to witness to those who have not heard the good news — the Gospel — and to point them to Christ. If

we fail to do this we will be held accountable
to God. We can witness by the words of our
mouth, by passing out tracts, or by sending
good Christian literature into their homes. If
we do not witness to the lost, we will have
their blood on our hands (Ezekiel 33:8).

The last command Jesus gave before he left
this earth was for his followers to not depart
from Jerusalem until they were baptized with
the Holy Spirit (See Acts 1:5). Then he said
they would receive power to be witnesses and
would go into all the world and preach the
Gospel (Acts 1:4-9; Mark 16:15-18). It was
not optional. It was a command to his
church. It still is!

If we want God to work for us, then we
should and must be willing to work for him!

Thousands of people know right from
wrong and they're not even born-again
Christians. Our God-given conscience even
tells us whether we're doing right or wrong,
unless it has become warped by dope, drink,
or the devil, so we can't think properly.
People know when they do wrong; that is

Want to please God

why they try to hide their sins. The closer we
get to God, the stronger and more sensitive ✗
our consciences get. That is why a child of
God who is close to God is very careful about
his actions, words, deeds and thoughts. He
wants to please God, because when you really
love someone, you trust them and you want
to please them and make them happy.

If we want to please God, we MUST
HAVE FAITH. *"But without faith it is impossible to please him" (Hebrews 11:6).*

Do you want to please God? Then have
faith in all of his Word, not just part of it.

Now here is the next "dose." It may seem
even harder to take than the last one we
mentioned. We have to TALK AS IF WE
HAVE THE ANSWER. You may say, "Well, I
can't do that. I can't say I have something
when I can't show it so people can see it; I
can't get myself out on a limb and make a
fool of myself."

But wait a minute! You didn't say it first. ✗

God said it first! He declared that we can
have *"WHATSOEVER WE SAY!" (Mark
11:23).* We have to say it, claim it out loud,
and stand on God's Word!

NOTE

His Word is the EVIDENCE that it is so!

We HAVE THE EVIDENCE!

Hebrews 11:1 states, *"Now faith is the substance of things hoped for, the EVIDENCE of things not seen."*

FAITH IS EVIDENCE!

Faith does not question. It knows!

If you really have faith, you KNOW YOU HAVE THE ANSWER and you can SAY IT — admit you already have the answer — even though at present it may be unseen by your mortal eyes.

It is the "evidence of things NOT SEEN." You don't have to see it first to have the evidence.

God's WORD IS THE EVIDENCE! Stand on it now and don't waver.

The answer is yours!

CHAPTER II

A Neglected Treasure

Turn in the Old Testament to the book of II Kings, chapter 4. Elisha was a prophet who was mightily anointed of God. He had a servant named Gehazi who was his right-hand man. In this chapter, three great miracles are recorded which Elisha performed because of his faith in God.

The first is the miracle of meeting the needs of a widow, or as we would say, the miracle of meeting a financial need. God is concerned about all our needs. He does not want us to live extravagantly or to be unwise in our spending, but he is a God of the material as well as of the spiritual needs, if we obey his laws.

This widow was about to have her two sons taken from her. It was a custom in those days for the creditor to come and take the children as slaves to pay off a debt that was owed to him if the debtor could not pay otherwise. Naturally she was scared and heartbroken. Since there were no public jobs for women in those days, it was impossible for her to seek employment, and perhaps she may have been too old to work anyway. Therefore, this woman faced a real dilemma. She was desperate, scared and hopeless until she remembered Elisha and his power to do miracles in the name of his Lord. She called Elisha, who had been the master of her deceased husband, and told him her problems. He said to her, *"What shall I do for thee? tell me, what hast thou in the house?" (II Kings 4:2).* She answered, *"Thine handmaid hath not any thing in the house, save a pot of oil."* Then he said, *"Go, borrow thee vessels abroad of all thy neighbors, even empty vessels; borrow not a few" (vs. 3).*

This precious handmaiden of the Lord did not question Elisha, she did not argue, she did not doubt. She merely obeyed! Up and down the streets and lanes she went, borrowing vessels from her neighbors. In the natural this may have seemed a foolish thing to do, but she didn't care. She was obeying the spokesman of God, for she believed God's Word.

Elisha continued his instructions which he had received from God. He then declared, *"And when thou art come in, thou shalt shut the door upon thee and upon thy sons, and shalt pour out into all those vessels, and thou shalt set aside that WHICH IS FULL."*

There are several things which we need to take note of here: Elisha said first, *"Borrow not a few."* In other words, DON'T LIMIT GOD! It is just as easy for God to do big things to meet big needs as it is to do little things to meet little needs. God can only be limited by our lack of faith! This woman could have borrowed a pot or two and quit believing, let her faith waver and stopped, but she obeyed and acted her faith. She didn't question Elisha and say, "Are you crazy? Do you think the little pot of oil that I have can fill all these vessels?"

We must remember that all through the Old Testament the oil was a type of the Holy Spirit. We fail to see miracles because we

underestimate the power of God's Holy
Spirit. We underestimate what he has given
us. If we have God, his Holy Spirit, and faith,
there is no limit to what we can do for God,
and we will see our own needs met. We have
to put that faith into action just as she put
her faith into action by gathering up the pots.

Now comes the next step. This is where
the miracle comes in. She began to pour. As
she poured, the oil began to multiply!

The more she poured, the more it multiplied!

The more it multiplied, the more she
poured!

It did not stop until the very last vessel
was full!

What a great spiritual treasure is found in
this lesson! The miracles come in the GIVING
OUT! The Lord promises in Luke 6:38:
"Give, and it shall be given unto you . . ." We
have to give of ourselves, of our means, of
our time, of our love, of our faith, of the
Word, and of the power of "oil" of the Holy
Spirit that has been placed within us. Unless
we give out, we will become stagnant and
dead in our experience with God.

The Holy Spirit is inexhaustible. God's supply can never run out. As long as there is an empty vessel into which we can give of the Holy Spirit and his blessings, it will continue flowing, but WE HAVE TO DO THE POURING! All God requires is that the vessels be clean. He will not pour his Spirit—his Holy Ghost Baptism—into an unclean or unsaved soul or vessel. It must first be cleansed by our faith in the shed blood of Christ and his forgiveness of our sins. Many people cannot be filled with God's Spirit because their old, ugly, selfish, carnal, doubting, sinful natures have not been changed.

The prophet continued, *"Thou shalt set aside that which is full."* He didn't want any half-empty vessels. When we are only half-full of God's presence and power, it leaves too much space for other things to enter that can pollute our experience and mar our relationship with God. We can only be a blessing to others when our own vessel is full and overflowing. A thirsty, dying world is out there just waiting to live on the overflow of God's Spirit in our lives. If we are only taking a little of God's power and presence, then we

can scarcely have enough for ourselves and no
surplus power to help others. Why limit God?
Bring your vessels, not a few!

A Careless Son Is Reproved

A story is told of a Christian father who
had become worried about his son who
seemed to be growing cold in his relationship
with God. The son hardly had time to read
his Bible and pray and attend church. He
entertained his carnal nature constantly with
other things. He began to associate with the
wrong crowd and read the wrong kind of
literature, and his faith in God had become
very weak. The father devised a plan. He
knew his son loved fresh fruit and candy bars,
so he saw that a huge bowl of these delicious
edibles was constantly set before his son. One
day the father took the lovely fruit bowl and
filled it with dirt and trash. On the top he
placed a few of the good things.

The son came in for his usual T.V. snack. He was shocked and angry to see the trash and dirt mixed in with the other goodies. He approached his father indignantly, demanding an explanation as to why he would do such a stupid trick. The father answered softly, "But son, you shouldn't mind the trash as long as there are some good things to eat among it." The son answered, "Oh yes, I should mind! The trash has contaminated the food and it is not fit to eat."

Then the father told his son that the fruit bowl with trash was placed there as an object lesson to let him know the condition of his mind. He stated, "While there may still be a few good things there, the 'trash' you've allowed to enter into your mind and heart has made the good things invalid and you are of no worth to God and his Kingdom." It was only then that the boy was able to comprehend what he had been allowing the devil to do to his mind and heart. He then repented and renewed his experience with God and set himself aside for the service of the Lord.

Our vessels must be full of God's presence if we would please him and see miracles in our lives and in the lives of others. We must be willing to pour out of our inner strength to help others. We can't have the fruit of the Spirit in our lives and at the same time have our minds cluttered with doubt and carnal things.

GOD CAN ONLY USE THOSE WHO ARE FULL OF HIS PRESENCE — THOSE WHO ARE WHOLLY DEDICATED TO HIM.

The prophet Elisha advised the woman to sell the oil and pay the debt she owed, so that she would no longer be held accountable for the debt which had been imposed upon her.

God's power, working in our lives, is enough not only to meet our needs, but to meet the needs of all those who come to us for God's help.

Great revival can only come to our churches when the "oil" of God's Holy Spirit begins to flow in individual lives!

Perhaps the most pertinent point of this story is that in the Bible, a pure woman is a type of the true church (Rev. 12). An adulterous woman is a type of the false church (Rev. 17).

The church, God's born-again believers, are the recipients of God's power when it meets the conditions which God stipulates. Unless there are sanctified vessels through whom the "oil" of the Holy Spirit can flow to meet the needs, the church will lose her sons and daughters. The enemy will take them from her. Cold or even lukewarm rituals and ceremonies are not the answer. If we would see a Holy Ghost revival and a genuine returning to God and the turn of the present tide of sin that is coming against, and sometimes even entering into, some of the church members, there must be first a genuine revival of SANCTIFICATION! This means not only the CLEANSING OF HEARTS FROM SIN, BUT ALSO THE SETTING APART OF VESSELS OR LIVES TO THE SERVICE OF GOD SO THEY CAN BE FILLED, THEN THAT OVERFLOW WILL REACH OUT TO THE LOST AND DYING! Mere religion cannot get the job done.

Another lesson from this story is that Elisha told her to shut her doors and shut herself in with her sons. Only when the church enters into her prayer closets with her sons and daughters and shuts out the world, or the worldly influences, will the power of God begin to flow to meet needs. The greatest need in the church today is not more talent, more eloquent speakers or entertainers, but more INTERCESSORY PRAYER WARRIORS—those who will shut themselves in with God for the needs of others as well as for themselves, and who will take dominion and authority over the enemy, the devil, and wrestle with him in the Spirit until he takes his flight.

Every father and mother MUST ESTABLISH FAMILY PRAYER IN THEIR HOMES and see to it that their children take part. If they fail to do this, their home will be sold out to the devil. Our children's Bible education should be as compulsory as their secular education unless we want to lose our sons and daughters to the devil! Are you selling your children out to the world and to the devil because you are too busy to take time to shut yourselves and them in with you and God?

Elisha continued, *"Pay thy debt, and live thou and thy children of the rest" (vs 7).* The church of the Lord Jesus Christ has a command to obey, a debt to pay. Christ died for us that we might be free, and free to serve.

> *Go ye into all the world, and preach the gospel to every creature. He that believeth and is baptized shall be saved; but he that believeth not shall be damned. And these signs shall follow them that believe; in my name shall they cast out devils; they shall speak with new tongues . . . They shall lay hands on the sick, and they SHALL RECOVER (Mark 16:15-18).*

THIS IS THE DEBT THAT THE CHURCH OWES — the responsibility to tell others the good news of salvation, sanctification, Holy Ghost baptism, healing and the Lord's soon coming, and the fact that the flow of God's "oil" of the Holy Spirit can meet every need. Then we, ourselves, can live the rest. After we have been faithful in obeying God's commandment, there will be enough left over to meet our needs, spiritually, financially and physically. But we must obey God's commandments, and do his works, serve him and put his work first.

How to Get Your Needs Met

We need to study the Bible very carefully. I've read the Bible for years and passed over important scriptures, or failed to comprehend their full meaning. Just as a person cannot be healthy without good, normal, healthy blood flowing in his veins, so the church cannot be spiritually healthy without the flow of God's Holy Spirit in the lives of the members.

Jesus spoke to me concerning the account of his feeding the five thousand in the 14th chapter of Matthew. When I read the part where Jesus said to his disciples, *"Give ye them to eat" (vs. 16),* God began to speak to me and tell me that the reason the disciples could not feed the people was because of their doubt. They were looking at the need instead of to the One who could meet that need. We have to get our eyes off of our needs and get them on Jesus. Peter walked on the water until he got his eyes off of Jesus, then he began to sink.

The disciples said, *"Send the multitude away" (vs. 15)*.

Jesus said, *"Feed them!"*

Jesus said to me, "Son, if my disciples had obeyed me when I commanded them, 'Give ye them to eat,' I would not have needed to touch the bread myself. They could have done it, but they doubted and wouldn't obey me!" They were looking at the circumstances just as Peter did, so they had to bring the bread to Jesus and let him perform the miracle because their doubt stopped the flow of the miraculous through them. God will not tell us to do anything that he will not qualify us to do! He would not ask us to feed the multitudes, or to serve those around about us if he did not intend to give us the power with which to do his work. His power to do all things is available to those who ASK AND BELIEVE! If we want God's power, we must be willing to feed others first.

Are you in debt so badly that you can't pay your bills? Is the devil trying to steal your children from you and wreck your home and ruin their lives? Have you gone to secular or worldly sources for help, or have you brought your needs to the man of God as this woman did? Not every one who professes to be God's servant or minister is truly God's anointed, but if he or she is living the right kind of life — a holy life — and has God's anointing, then God demands that we have respect for them. Lots of even so-called "full gospel" people will go to some human force or some carnal friend before they will go to a man or woman of God for help. This is putting God's power second, instead of first as it should be.

I want to show you that God still works through his servants. We had a boy sitting in the audience in one of my meetings who tried to kill himself. He was devil-possessed. He had tried to take his own life several times. The last time he tried this he was kept in the hospital for four days and nights as he was unconscious. He had gone from pastor to pastor, and from state to state, trying to get someone to cast these things out of him, but he said they would just pat him on the back and say, "Well, we'll be praying for you." He tried to kill himself again and was put in a mental institution. I prayed and commanded the demons to go in the name of Jesus Christ, and they had to leave because of my faith in the power of that great name!

Where did you go the last time YOU needed help? Did you go to a powerless source, or did you go to a man of God? You can't get help from people who are just religious professors. You have to go to someone who believes in the full gospel, who believes in the power of God and has it manifested in his life. I don't claim to know everything the Bible says, but thank God, I do know enough of what it says to bring deliverance to others in the name of our Lord. It is not how much we know, but HOW MUCH WE PUT INTO PRACTICE THAT REALLY COUNTS!

What God did in the Old Testament, he will do in the New Testament, and what he did in the New Testament, he has given us authority to do today.

God never changes!

He is interested in your financial needs just as much as he was in feeding the five thousand in the New Testament.

He is just as interested in his children today as he was then.

What he did yesterday, he can still do today.

God hasn't changed, nor will he ever!

It is we who have changed.

If you are attending a church which doesn't believe in miracles and whose leaders say that miracles are not for today, then you had better find a different church because they will destroy your faith.

A Young Man Was Healed Of Cancer

There was a young man in one of my meetings who was Spirit-filled, and yet he was dying with cancer. Through the preaching of the Word, his faith took hold of God's promises and as I prayed for him, he was healed. Medical science has not yet found a cure for cancer though millions of dollars are being spent in research, but no disease can stand before God's mighty power if we only have faith to believe!

Many people say, "I know God has the power to do it, but will he?" Let me ask you a question: If someone came to you who was suffering or in a helpless condition, would you help him or her? Of course you would, if you are a true child of God. Do you think that you are more righteous or loving than God? Then why not trust him and his Word?

Did you ever invite anyone into your house to give them a bed and to give them food? I have. In fact, I'd be afraid to turn them away unless God showed me that they had come to harm me. But if they are honest and trying to work for God, I wouldn't dare close my heart of compassion against them. If we care about others, then how much more does God care about us? He will never say "no" to something we really need or that is best for us, if our faith meets his test.

Let us digress from these thoughts again and go back and consider the prophet Elisha.

First, let me remind you that he was a servant of the great prophet Elijah. We must first be servants if we would later be leaders, and we must first have a teachable spirit, if we would later be qualified to teach. Elisha followed Elijah as he performed all kinds of miracles. There were many other sons of the prophets who had training under Elijah, but they weren't really interested in carrying on the work of God and in having God's power in their lives so as to be able to help others. Elisha was. His constant prayer was not only to have the anointing as Elijah had, but to have a double portion. He didn't let go until he got his request. As Elijah was being caught up and carried into heaven in a fiery chariot sent from God, his mantle, a type of God's power and anointing, fell upon Elisha, so he continued the work of God, carrying on the ministry of Elijah or the ministry of the Holy Ghost through Elijah. If we want the "mantle" of God's power to fall on us today, we will have to first contend for it!

Because Elisha was a servant of God, God moved on the heart of a woman, whom the Bible declared was a great woman (II Kings

4:8) to take care of his needs. She had her husband build him a special room and resting place, and they fed him when he came that way. Again I say, if we will do God's work and put him first, God will take care of our own needs. The love of God is like a boomerang. When you throw it out, it always comes back to you. You can't give out the love of God, or money or time to others without having it come back to you in one form or another. It may be in good health, or spiritual or financial blessings, or in true friendship and love from others. Whatever the case may be, it will return, for God's law of sowing and reaping is irrevocable.

Elisha, God's prophet, appreciated so much what this woman and her husband had done for him and his servant Gehazi that he wanted to do something to show his appreciation. Gehazi suggested that since she had never been able to have children that Elisha could pray that she would become a mother. The Spirit of the Lord came upon Elisha and he called her and told her that at the same time the following year she would be embracing a son in her arms. Sometimes false prophets will prophesy things from their own minds and spirits. We must take heed to whom we listen and in whom we trust. No man can know the future except through the supernatural anointing and power of the Holy Ghost.

Elisha was a true prophet of God, so his prophecy was fulfilled. He knew that he was serving the same God that caused Sarah to conceive and bear Isaac when she was ninety and her husband, Abraham, was a hundred years old. He also knew that God is no respecter of persons.

But this promise from the man of God was too much or too good for this Shunammite woman to believe. She said, *"Nay, my lord, thou man of God, do not lie unto thine handmaid."* This woman, in looking at things from the natural standpoint had reason to doubt as her husband also was very old, and it upset her very much to think that Elisha would joke with her about a matter that meant so much to her.

God can do things for us that will "stagger" our imagination if we only believe! It was just a small thing for our Great Creator to renew and rejuvenate the bodies of these faithful people. What seems as a mountain to us is no more than a speck to our great omnipotent God!

Life In The Face Of Death

The 17th verse of the 4th chapter of II Kings states, *"And the woman conceived, and bare a son at that season that Elisha had said unto her, according to the time of life."* God is not slack concerning his promises. Even if we need a miracle of creation such as new organs, new hearts, or new limbs, it is a small thing with God. Only he can create! Creation is just one of his many daily "chores," but to the finite mind it is a miracle almost too great to comprehend or to believe.

For three years I struggled and prayed to believe the Bible, but it seemed at first that I just couldn't. I had to undo some wrong thinking so as to be able to believe the right

things. I was a staunch member of the First
Baptist Church. I had never ever seen a
cripple healed; neither had I seen any other
miracles that happened in the Bible. I hadn't
heard it preached that it was possible, or even
likely for our present day. I cried out to God
and said, "God, I want to believe it, but I
just can't! I can't even believe the Bible!" I
cried out even louder in my frustration and
said, "Help me, God, I want to believe it, but
I just can't!" That was my First Baptist mind
expressing itself.

For three long years I wondered about it in
my confused mind. I prayed for God to
touch my mind so I could believe the Bible. I
would read it, but I just couldn't believe that
those miracles were still for us today. Then I
read where the Bible states, *"For I am the
Lord, I change not;" (Mal. 3:6)* and *"Jesus
Christ, the same yesterday, today, and for-
ever,"* and other such verses, but still it was
hard to believe. I was a born-again Christian. I
believed in salvation through Christ, but I just
couldn't seem to believe in the miraculous.

Because of my unbelief in the past, it is
easy for me to relate to the Shunammite

woman's unbelief and to understand why she thought Elisha was lying to her. You might say, "Well, I guess that was the end of her troubles," but it wasn't. God had even a greater miracle to perform for this woman, but she had to go through a very sad experience first. Did you ever stop to realize that sometimes our disappointments are God's appointments? They give God a chance to perform a miracle. Miracles are only performed when there is a great need beyond the help of human ability, so sometimes our own efforts have to be exhausted before God can step in and take over!

A Young Man is Brought Back to Life

In the 4th chapter of II Kings the Scriptures tell us that when this woman's son was grown that he suddenly had a terrible headache, then he died shortly afterwards. What would you do if this happened to your child?

I suppose you would just call the funeral home, for that is the "normal" thing to do. God doesn't just deal in the normal because he is not confined to the normal. He is a supernatural God, so he does supernatural things! Super means above. God's power and ways are so much higher than ours that it is hard for us natural, normal people to believe in the supernatural.

It takes "funny" or peculiar people, God's people, who would rather attend church or read his Word or pray, or go out and witness to the lost and dying, than to be entertained by a ball game or a sensual T.V. program. It takes so-called "odd" people like us, who supposedly have gone off the "deep end," to believe God for the miraculous. Why? Because we live in a different "world" or spiritual realm. We live in a world (mental state) where the Spirit of God within us controls our lives and takes first place, instead of a world where the carnal, fleshly desires and appetites take control or precedence. If we want to see God as he really is, in his power to do miracles, then we have to get on a higher plane than those who are merely "religious" people, or the unsaved who live and behave like animals.

God will give his children whatever they need and want if they will only believe. Creating new parts for a body is no problem for him; raising the dead is no problem for him, for he was the giver of life from the beginning. The problem is not in him. If we fail to believe, it is in us! He declared, *"For with God nothing shall be impossible" (Luke 1:37).* He meant exactly what he said. He was not joking or lying!

If your faith is weak, then hunt up a man of God and get him to believe with you. That is why the Bible states that *"if two of you shall agree on earth as touching any thing that they ask, IT SHALL BE DONE..." (Matthew 18:19).* Sometimes it is good to pray with someone else who also has great faith, as we can be inspired by another person's faith, so that our own faith will be increased.

Resurrection Faith!

Notice the faith of this woman in II Kings 4:21-23. She didn't become hysterical; she didn't start screaming and weeping. She just calmly laid the youth in the bed of Elisha, then she told one of the young men to drive fast and take her to the man of God. Her husband may have been terribly upset, but she said to him, "It shall be well."

Here are two great keys that are top secrets in getting healing from God, and he told me to point them out to you.

First, notice again there was ACTIVE FAITH!

Second, SHE CONFESSED HER FAITH OUT LOUD WITH HER MOUTH! She said, "IT SHALL BE WELL," not maybe, or I hope so, or I think so, but it shall be! What a positive statement! There was nothing negative about her actions or her speech. She knew that the God who had given life to her and her husband's body so this child could be born was the same God that would give his life back.

THIS IS RESURRECTION FAITH!

Remember it was Mary who sat at the feet of Jesus who had resurrection faith when Lazarus lay in the tomb, while it was her sister Martha, always too encumbered with much serving or the material things of life, who had lost all hope (St. John 11).

God was testing her faith to see if it would hold out. In school, before each promotion, there has to be a test given. It has to be passed with satisfactory results or grades. Before God can promote us to a higher realm of faith, he has to test our actions to see if we're measuring up to his Word! He had to test her to see if she had faith according to Hebrews 11:1.

She passed the test! Notice how Elisha said, *"Run now, I pray thee, to meet her, and say unto her, ". . . Is it well with the CHILD?"* She answered and said, *"IT IS WELL" (II Kings 4:26).* How many of us could say it is well with our child if he or she was a cold corpse? If we said that, people would probably think we had gone crazy or just didn't care that our child had died. This woman was not looking to circumstances, but she was looking to the resurrection power of God that she knew would be manifested through Elisha.

God wants us to have the faith of Abraham and that means that we will look right up to

God and call things that be not as though
they were. That is God faith! "Strong medicine" again you may say, but if we'll take it
as prescribed and get all those "bugs" of
doubt out of our spiritual system, we'll be
healed of our doubt and unbelief, then we'll
be ready to do the works of Christ, and also
to receive for ourselves.

Jesus said that he did not his works, but
the works of the Father who sent him. He
later declared that if we believe on him and
his works, then we would do greater works
because he was going to his Father (St. John
14:12). This meant greater in quantity, not in
quality, for his church is many. He was
limited to one body when he was on this
earth, but now we are his vessels through
whom he works as extensions of his hands!

The devil has been cunning in getting lots
of people to believe that God is dead. That is
why he hates miracles. It makes people know
that God is still alive when God does the
supernatural, and it helps people to realize
that he is a supernatural God who really cares
and loves his creation. Satan isn't worried
about the social, lukewarm, miracle-denying

preacher, but he does get worried when people start believing God and acting on his Word, because his wicked kingdom of darkness is being shaken and torn down. That is why the devil attacks every man and woman of God who dares to believe God.

They are as generals or captains in God's army, so they are prime targets. If he can't find some weak spot to put a wedge into and get them to fail God and fall, then he gets his evil servants to start a bunch of lies to cause people to doubt those in whom God has entrusted his power. This is why we must be *NOTE* very careful not to believe things of a malicious or defamatory nature against a person until they are proven. God said, *"Touch not mine anointed, and do my prophets no harm" (I Chron. 16:22).* Even well-meaning people have allowed themselves to become instruments of the devil in repeating things which are not true. God recently spoke to a woman of God, a dedicated prayer warrior, and told her that an invasion of lying demons would take place and that their attacks had already begun. He told her that these attacks would be so insidious that unless God's servants stood their ground and bound these spirits in the name of Jesus that confidence of people in general in the things of God would be so shaken that many would become discouraged and fall away from God and would even become enemies of the church and of God's children. Also, that God's work would be greatly hindered by this terrible onslaught unless God's people come against these lying spirits and take authority over them and bind them and their evil influence.

If you are prone to doubt this revelation which was given to this woman, you only have to turn on your T.V. sets for a short time to sacrilegious films which are portraying our beautiful Lord as a sinful, lustful man, or to see constant attacks on the church by their portraying all Christians as hypocrites. These atheistic, malicious attacks will become more and more frequent unless God's people unite to do something about them.

In the face of seeming death, the Shunammite woman said, *"It is well!"*

Do you want things to be well at your house! If you do, say out loud, by faith, "It is well! It is well!" Say and claim it in the name of Jesus Christ.

Say, "It is well at my house."

You may think, "Now this is really strong medicine to take. How can I say it is well when everything seems to be going wrong, and when I have all kinds of problems? Wouldn't that be lying?"

Let me ask you, are you going to believe the lies of the devil or the truths and promises of God? You have to believe one of them. God says, "It is well." The devil says, "You're defeated; give up." Now whom will you believe?

Jesus said in Mark 11:23,

> *that whosoever shall SAY unto this mountain, Be thou removed, and be thou cast into the sea; and SHALL NOT DOUBT IN HIS HEART . . . shall have whatsoever he SAITH.*

By faith, rebuke the devil in Jesus' name and command him to take his hands off of you and your family and say out loud, "IT IS WELL."

Continue to believe it and it will be.

Notice the woman caught Elisha by his feet. She wouldn't let him go (II Kings 4:27).

By this she was saying, "I'll hold on to the promises and power of God. I will not accept defeat! I will not accept death! I will not let go of God's power!"

Jacob wrestled with an angel all night and told him that he would not let go until the angel blessed him. The angel had to change Jacob's nature BEFORE HE COULD GRANT JACOB'S REQUEST! Sometimes God has to first do a spiritual work in our lives before he can answer our prayers. The name Jacob meant "deceiver." Jacob was determined to get that which he needed from God. God changed his nature, and consequently his name, to "Israel" which means "a prince of God."

God's cleansing and sanctifying power can change our very natures and put the royal blood of Christ in our veins, which is the new birth by the Holy Spirit, and then we become as princes, kings, princesses and queens of God. In other words, we become royal stock and of the royal class, spiritually speaking. We become heirs of his throne, and shall rule and reign with him (Rev. 20). Real estate will be no problem, for we will inherit the mansions which he has gone away to build for us (John 14:1-3).

But the greatest and most wonderful of all is that we become heirs of his power (Luke 10:19), and that includes the authority to take dominion and power over "ALL THE POWER OF THE ENEMY." This great fact should relieve us of any future fear or worry. Hallelujah! Our victory is complete through Christ!

The Shunammite woman had every right in the world to demand that the prophet come to the rescue of her son as she and her husband had tended to his needs and given of their substance so he could carry on the work of God. If we give to God's cause and kingdom, and live as good representatives of what we teach and preach, we have every right to come to Christ in our time of need. God's Word tells us to *"COME BOLDLY UNTO THE THRONE OF GRACE" IN TIME OF NEED (Hebrews 4:16).* We are not to come as beggars, but as his royal children, who have been redeemed by his blood and made heirs of his great Kingdom.

If you are a child of God, come boldly in prayer right now before him, then thank him and claim the answer.

If you have not accepted him as your Lord and Savior, do so right now. Confess your sins to him and ask his forgiveness.

Praise him and thank him, and claim him as your Savior.

CHAPTER III

A Pauper Becomes an Heir

A very touching love story has been told about a handsome prince in Scotland who had everything his heart could desire. He and his servants would often ride up into the Highlands to hunt. His beautiful, white steed, with its silver and gold harness could often be seen dashing and flashing in the sun as he swiftly bore his master on a big fox chase. One day the young prince saw in the distance a peasant farm house that was burning. He abruptly called a halt to the hunt and went to investigate. Coming nearer, he saw that it was too late to save the humble cottage of the poor peasant family, but he was moved with compassion as he heard the pitiful screams of the crippled mother who declared that her young daughter had been trapped inside. Not thinking of his own safety, the royal young prince quickly dismounted and ran into the flames and rescued the beautiful young maiden.

Years later the girl, who had grown to full maturity, came to the village to attend school. One day as she was walking down the street, the young prince noticed her, and not knowing who she was, asked her for a date, and he soon fell deeply in love with her and asked her to become his wife. Because of the girl's poverty-stricken background, she wouldn't make her identity known, and refused to marry him. When he became more and more persistent, she finally admitted to him that she was only the daughter of the poorest of peasants, but to her surprise, his love for her was so great that her impecuniosity mattered little to him.

On the day of their wedding, before the ceremony, he came to her with a sad look on his face. He said, "I have a secret which I have kept from you. Now I must tell you." Her heart almost stopped beating. She thought to herself, "Now I know. He must have reconsidered and decided that he does not really love me, or that he can't marry me because I am a peasant's daughter, and not of royal stock such as he." But, to her surprise, he said, "My darling, my love grows greater for you each day, but I have to let you know my secret." Then he pulled off his gloves, which he had always worn on their dates, as it was the custom for princes to do, and showed her two ugly, scarred hands. He said, "I had to be fair and let you see these before I married you as you might not want me with deformed hands. You see, this happened one day when I was hunting in the Highlands and a peasant's house was on fire. I rushed in, risking my life, and rescued a young girl from the burning flames. But if you still want to marry me, I will love you always and make you an heir of all that I have."

The young girl let out a scream, rushed into his arms and took his hands and started kissing them over and over again. She then looked up at him, with tears streaming down her cheeks and said, "My darling, I love you now more than ever. I'm the cause of those scars. I'm the young girl of the peasant family whom you saved that day." With that they fell into each other's arms, wept and embraced each other, and went into the marriage chamber.

It is because of his love for us that Jesus has the scars in his hands, his feet and his side. He died to save us from a burning hell and to make us heirs of his love and power and of eternal life (John 3:16).

According to the 13th and 14th chapters of Zechariah, when he returns to set up his kingdom for the millennial reign, he will still have those scars in his hands. We, who were paupers spiritually speaking, have become heirs of God and joint-heirs with Christ (Romans 8:17; Gal. 4:7). But with that heirship comes also a responsibility to extol his name, to help build his great kingdom on earth, and to serve others by continuing the works which he began. To do this we must first take God's "medicine" of faith as prescribed, and be bold in standing on his promises.

This is why we can say, "It is well."

It is well because Jesus paid it all. In Jesus' dying for our salvation, we, by faith, become

God's children and his heirs. This includes the right to use Jesus' authority and his name to take dominion over demon spirits, over diseases, to lay hands on the sick, to pray for others to be saved, delivered, baptized with the Holy Spirit, and to be protected from evils that would come against us. Yes, and even to raise the dead! (Mark 16:15-18 and John 14:12-17).

"It is well" because Jesus made it well! By faith in his power and his works, according to these Scriptures, we can declare things "well" and they will be, but we must do as the Shunammite woman did. Even in the face of the hardest trials we must declare that the victory is ours through Christ.

"IT IS WELL!"

There Is No Substitute For God's Power

Notice verse 30, II Kings, 4. She said, *"As the Lord liveth, and as thy soul liveth, I WILL NOT LEAVE THEE."*

When we reject Christ and the baptism in the Holy Spirit, we reject our only source of power. Elisha had tried to comfort her by sending his servant in his place, but nothing happened. The child remained cold and dead. This woman was wise enough to know that Gehazi, the servant, did not have God's power, so she would NOT ACCEPT A SUBSTITUTE. She clung to Elisha until she got the answer.

We must never accept a substitute for God's power. It will always fail. There is no real substitute for God's power. It can't be substituted by mere pretense, or just religion, or by programs or talent. It must come directly from God and he must have ALL THE GLORY IF WE WOULD HAVE RESULTS!

Samson flirted and played around with Delilah, a type of the world, until he lost his power. He tried to fool and deceive the people of Israel by pretending he still had God's power and anointing resting upon him, but he was only deceiving himself, for they soon found out the truth. He got by for awhile on his past reputation and success, but it didn't last long. We may fool the people for awhile, but we never can fool God. It pays to keep our prayer life up and our lamps trimmed and burning with the "oil" of the Holy Spirit.

David, a man of God's own heart, who had won very great victories, failed God and committed a terrible sin because he was napping spiritually when he should have been praying for those who were fighting Israel's battles on the front line. There is no substitute for God's power; neither is there anything that can take the place of our prayer life if we would have this power!

Just as there are no substitutes, there are also no short cuts. We have a price to pay and that is in DILIGENTLY SEEKING GOD. Like the woman who clung to Elisha, we must not let go until God blesses us and anoints us, and empowers us for his service. Without this, we may rise and "shake" ourselves as Samson did when the enemy was upon him, only to find that our spiritual strength is gone.

If we do not keep the laws and commandments of God and live according to his

Word, and believe and act upon it, we will become as powerless as the substitute, Gehazi, who failed to get the job done.

In chapter 5, we read where Gehazi lied and tried to deceive Naaman so he could have the gold for himself which Elisha had rejected as payment for God's power in healing Naaman. The Lord revealed this to Elisha, and Gehazi was smitten with leprosy, the same disease of which Naaman was healed. When the gift of the word of knowledge such as Elisha had, and which is available for God's true servants today, begins to work in the lives of God's children, people will have to pray through and get the real thing or their hypocrisy will be exposed. (see I Cor. 12:7-12).

If we sell out for lusts of the flesh, or for money, or prestige, or for power, we will become useless and futile substitutes and God cannot use us to do his work, and the leprosy of sin will sooner or later consume us and all that we have. Gehazi's household was even smitten with this incurable disease as the results of his disobedience and sins. Our families can be lost because of our failing

God. Let us take heed and not sell out for any carnal desire.

Like the Shunammite woman, we must contend for the real thing — the real faith — the real presence and power of God. We must live holy lives so that God's presence and power will meet our needs. We must say as she did, "I WILL NOT LEAVE THEE." There is no power like God's power, no love like his love and no mercy like his mercy, but we must live in his favor to obtain it.

There is still another very important factor which needs to be brought to your attention. Notice in the 33rd verse that he went in and prayed for the child, but at first nothing happened. Then God said he WANTED ACTION! Notice in the 34th verse how Elisha went into action. It states: *"And he went up, and lay upon the child, and put his mouth upon his mouth, and his eyes upon his eyes, and his hands upon his hands: and he stretched himself upon the child; and the flesh of the child waxed warm."* The next verse states: *"Then he . . . walked to and fro."* No doubt he was praising God for the answer. Then he *"went up, and stretched himself upon him: and the child sneezed seven times, and the child opened his eyes."*

Notice that sometimes Christ heals instantly, but sometimes he is waiting for certain conditions to be met by the individual. When there is nothing in the way such as unbelief or an unforgiving spirit, or any such thing that would hinder the flowing of the Spirit, the healing is usually instant, and that is a miracle.

When Jesus was on earth, most of the time he healed instantly. However, there were a few times when he healed gradually. He has power to heal instantly every time, but his power is released according to our faith.

In the 5th chapter of St. Mark, when Jesus and his disciples went into the country of the Gadarenes, they immediately encountered a mad man. He lived among the tombs. His wild, hideous screaming and crying scared the people, but no man or group of men could bind him, for he was too strong. He cut himself with sharp stones and tried to take his life. The demon was forced to acknowledge that he and many others were present in the man and were the cause of all his trouble.

The demon said, *"My name is Legion, for we are many" (Mark 5:9).*

Jesus had a reason for doing this. He wasn't deliberately delaying because of any lack of faith or power. He wanted his disciples and the people of that country to realize that he not only had power to heal diseases, to restore blind eyes, to open deaf ears, to meet the needs of the hungry, and to raise the dead, but that HE, THE SON OF GOD, HAS POWER OVER THE DEVIL AND HIS DEMON SPIRITS!

Jesus defeated Satan at Calvary. He then went down into the heart of the earth and wrestled the keys of death, hell and the grave from him. He arose from the dead and gave the keys of power and authority to the church, the truly born-again believers OF ALL AGES, INCLUDING OURS. He has not relinquished that power, but continues to invest it in those who sincerely believe.

The demon said that his name was Legion. A legion of troops in that day consisted of from 4,200 to 6,000 men, so we can speculate there were at least 4,000 demons in this man, driving and tormenting him. Regardless of how powerful Satan is, Christ is still stronger and he is the victor in all situations when we meet his conditions. Sometimes when people are brought for healing or for salvation, the demons which control their bodies and minds have to first be cast out. Too often when God heals a person, the healing doesn't last because the person healed allows the demons to come back. If unforgiveness, bitterness, resentment or some other attitude has given a foothold to the devil, our attitudes must be changed to prevent the demonic attacks on our minds.

> *When the unclean spirit is gone out of a man, he walketh through dry places seeking rest, and findeth none. Then he saith, I will return into my house from whence I came out; and when he is come, he findeth it empty, swept, and garnished. Then goeth he, and taketh with himself seven other spirits more wicked than himself, and they enter in and dwell there: and the last state*

> *of that man is worse than the*
> *first. Even so shall it be also*
> *unto this wicked generation*
> *(Matt. 12:43-45).*

Jesus also wanted to teach his disciples, who would carry on his work after he went back to the Father, how to bring deliverance to the demon-possessed. He will teach you today if you will read the gospels and the book of Acts, and take authority in his name. It is the responsibility of the church to cast out demons. It isn't optional: it is a direct COMMAND! (Mark 16:17). This may also be strong "medicine" to take, but it was one of Jesus' last orders before he ascended to heaven. Unless his church, God's children who have been redeemed, obey this command, it will never be done and the possessed will be eternally lost.

Notice how the woman fell at Elisha's feet and thanked him after her child was restored to life. The Bible tells us, *"In every thing give thanks: for this is the will of God in Christ Jesus concerning you" (I Thess. 5:18).* Again this verse may seem to be strong "medicine," as it is very hard for us to be thankful when everything seems to be going wrong. But if your faith is strong, it is easy to look just above the clouds into the face of Jesus and thank God because he knows and understands, and will soon change things if our faith does not waver. This woman fell at the prophet's feet before she went over and took the child up in her arms, then she took her son and departed.

Remember that faith sees the answer spiritually before the human eyes actually see it. This woman said, "It is well," BEFORE she saw the boy walking and talking. This is the message that God has been trying to get across to his church for almost two thousand years! We must learn to stand on God's Word without wavering, and praise the Lord for the answer even if it seems at present that all heaven has turned to brass.

Don't halfway pray a few times, then walk off discouraged and say, "It must not have been God's will after all." Don't you worry about God's will. The Bible is God's will! It is your will that God has to work with.

God's will is to bring life and health into your family; also to bring happiness and peace.

God's will is for you to be successful and prosperous, but you must not forget he has rules by which you have to operate. You must take the spiritual "medicine" which he prescribes. We can't just be "fair-weather" Christians. We have to learn to trust him and praise him in the time of stormy trials and testings, knowing that these will draw us closer to him.

A Proud Heart Receives Nothing

Notice the "medicine" that proud Naaman had to take before he was cleansed. Elisha wouldn't even go to the door and speak to him although Naaman was a man of prestige, and had brought him much silver and gold and other expensive gifts. Elisha told his servant to tell him to go dip in the Jordan River seven times and he would be cleansed of his leprosy. Naaman was indignant; he felt insulted. Why should he, the famous, honorable captain of the host of Syria, have to dip in an old muddy river? How could there be healing in such?

At first he refused and went away in a rage, but his wise servants came to him and said, *"My father, if the prophet had bid thee do some great thing, wouldest thou not have done it? how much rather then, when he saith to thee, Wash, and be clean?" (II Kings 5:13).* Naaman reconsidered and obeyed and was immediately healed. His flesh became like unto the flesh of a little child (vs. 14). He wanted to put on a big show and do something real big, but these motives did not please God, so God prompted Elisha to require Naaman to do something that was very humiliating. That seemed to be strong "medicine" for Naaman's pride, but he had to take it as prescribed before God could perform the miracle.

God deals with the rich and the poor alike; he has no double standards!

Jesus has all kinds of ways of meeting people's needs; because he has all kinds of people with whom to deal. Some have to be delivered of envy, of a gossiping tongue, or of a proud or unforgiving spirit. Others have to

Good

be encouraged to believe that they are worthy to receive, as they feel inferior to others and unworthy to receive anything. God has to deal with people according to their personality and emotional and spiritual condition before he can meet their physical, financial and spiritual needs.

The Answer Is Yours

Jesus told his disciples on one occasion to go fishing and they found a coin in a fish's mouth with which to pay their taxes. If someone went fishing today, expecting to get his taxes paid that way, he'd probably be turned out of the church for being a fanatic, or maybe he would be considered insane. Jesus has all kinds of ways to answer our prayers. It is not ours to worry about as to how, but to only believe and ACT.

Jesus wants action!

Our faith must be active in order to receive from God. Jordan means "downpour." There were no healing qualities in that river. The healing of Naaman came as he acted out his faith, then the downpour of God's blessings came.

Just as healing was provided for those in the Old Testament as they met God's conditions, so healing is also provided in the New

This pg. good explanation

Testament, or the new covenant. James 5:14 states: *"Is any sick among you? let him call for the elders of the church; and let them pray over him, anointing him with oil IN THE NAME OF THE LORD: And the prayer of FAITH shall save the sick, and the Lord shall raise him up; and if he have committed sins, they shall be forgiven him" (vs. 15).*

Spiritual and physical healing go hand in hand. It is so vital that we stay out of sin if we expect Jesus to keep us healthy. He doesn't heal people so they can go serve the devil. The oil is a type of God's Holy Spirit. The oil has no healing qualities of its own, just as the Jordan River had none. It is the act of obedience and faith that brings the results; and it is the real oil, the power of the Holy Spirit which heals.

In St. Mark 1:40 in the New Testament we have recorded the healing of another leper. Jesus cleansed him and made him whole when the leper knelt before him, worshipping him and declared his faith in Christ's power to heal. Worship and faith must precede anything that we receive from God!

Jesus promised, *"Lo, I am with you alway, even unto the end of the world" (Matt.*

28:20). Jesus is with you right now just as much as he was when he walked the shores of Galilee when he cleansed the lepers and raised the dead. He has not changed! Wherever and whenever his Word, WHETHER WRITTEN OR SPOKEN, IS ACTED UPON IN FAITH, THE ANSWER WILL COME!

NOTE

A very famous, international evangelist, while preaching overseas, was trying to get the people to believe this promise. During the service, great miracles took place in the name of Jesus as people began to believe and act on the Word of God. One man came forward who had been suffering during the service with three broken ribs. He testified that suddenly he saw the Lord standing before him in a beautiful white robe. He said, "Jesus then smiled at me and put his hands on my ribs. A warmth went through my chest and I was suddenly relieved of all pain and instantly healed."

In another place a poor insane beggar was healed and restored to his right mind. As we prayed in Jesus' name, suddenly the old beggar saw the Lord. He said the Lord looked at him, and pointed his fingers at him and spoke to the demons which possessed him and said, "Come out of the man!" The people there rejoiced greatly as they witnessed these and many other miracles which were done in the name and through the power of Jesus.

Believe right there where you are. Search your heart and see if you need to first apply any of the "medicine" scriptures of God's Word which have been presented in this book.

If you do, humble yourself before God and believe for inward or outward healing. If it is a financial problem, or family problems, or other needs, worship the Lord out loud and praise him for the answer.

BY FAITH, IT IS YOURS RIGHT NOW!

BOOKS AND TAPES BY NORVEL HAYES

Please order from the following and enclose check or money order with each order:

> NORVEL HAYES
> CAMPUS CHALLENGE MISSIONS
> P. O. BOX 1379
> CLEVELAND, TENN. 37311
> Attention: Order Enclosed

Please add 50¢ postage & handling for orders under $10.

Thank you.

BOOKS BY NORVEL HAYES:

YOUR FAITH CAN HEAL YOU.........................$1.00
JESUS TAUGHT ME TO CAST OUT DEVILS....1.25
GOD'S POWER THROUGH LAYING ON
   OF HANDS...1.25
HOW TO PROTECT YOUR FAITH.....................1.95

BIBLE TEACHING CASSETTE TAPES
BY NORVEL HAYES:

Prices		
	1 tape	$ 3.95
	3 tapes	10.00
	12 tapes	34.00
ALL 92 tapes		220.00

1   SPEAK THE WORD ONLY

2   READ, BELIEVE, AND ACT, SAITH THE LORD

3   PROPHECY

4   THE CHURCH, THE ROCK

5   HOW TO GET YOUR PRAYERS ANSWERED

6   GOD'S POWER

7   IT IS WRITTEN

8   YOUR FAITH BRINGS VICTORY

9   'BUILD YOUR FAITH

10   DON'T TWIST GOD'S WORD

11   GOD'S HEALING POWER

12   BAPTISM OF THE HOLY SPIRIT BY FAITH

13   HEALING OF THE NERVES

14   THREE POWER GIFTS OF THE SPIRIT

15   THREE VOCAL GIFTS OF THE SPIRIT

16   THREE REVELATION GIFTS OF THE SPIRIT

17   FIVE STEPS OF DELIVERANCE FOR THE CHRISTIAN